Time
at Home

Meg and Steven Roberts

PHOTOGRAPHS BY Maura McEvoy
TEXT BY Brenda Cullerton

Time at Home

HARRY N. ABRAMS, INC., PUBLISHERS

Editor
Elisa Urbanelli
Designer
Henk van Assen

Library of Congress Cataloging-in-Publication Data

Roberts, Meg Lesser.
    Time at home/Meg Lesser Roberts and Steven Roberts ;
    text by Brenda Cullerton ; photographs by Maura McEvoy.
    p.   cm.

    ISBN 0–8109–4497–9
    1. Interior decoration—Psychological aspects.
    I. Roberts, Steven, 1956– II. Cullerton, Brenda. III. Title.
    NK2113 .R62 2001
    747'.01'9—dc21
                                            2001001266

Harry N. Abrams, Inc.
100 Fifth Avenue
New York, N.Y. 10011
www.abramsbooks.com

Interior Design Credits
Linda Banks: 38–39, 84; Laurin Copen, The Rose House Antiques
Market: 22, 24, 48, 75, 97, 102; Jeanne-Aelia Desparmet-Hart, JADH
design, Larchmont, N.Y.: 99, 101, 109; Donna Francis: 12–13, 18, 19, 31,
94, 95; Karen Gilliatt: 36–37, 111; Susan Hager: 53, 67, 89; John David
Hunter, Washington Depot, Conn.: 43, 83, 88, 122; Michael Johnston:
104, 105; Christine Lambert Layton: 46, 108, 121 (also designed
fabrics); Claudia Librett: 119; Stephen Mallory: 35, 92, 93, 100, 103;
Amanda Moffat: 77, 90–91; Jennifer Pendry: 34, 44, 74; Kevin Walz:
126; Richard White: 29, 30, 64, 79

Photograph Credits
All photographs by Maura McEvoy except the following: William Boyd:
128; Adrianne dePolo: 15; Meg Roberts: 10–11, 127

Architecture Credits
Fifield Piaker & Associates Architects: 45, 62, 63; Page Goolrick
Architects: 32, 51

Artwork Credits
Art Gate: 25, 116–117; Sandi Fifield: 62, 63; Steve Miller: 54, 55, 112;
Joyce Seymore: 80

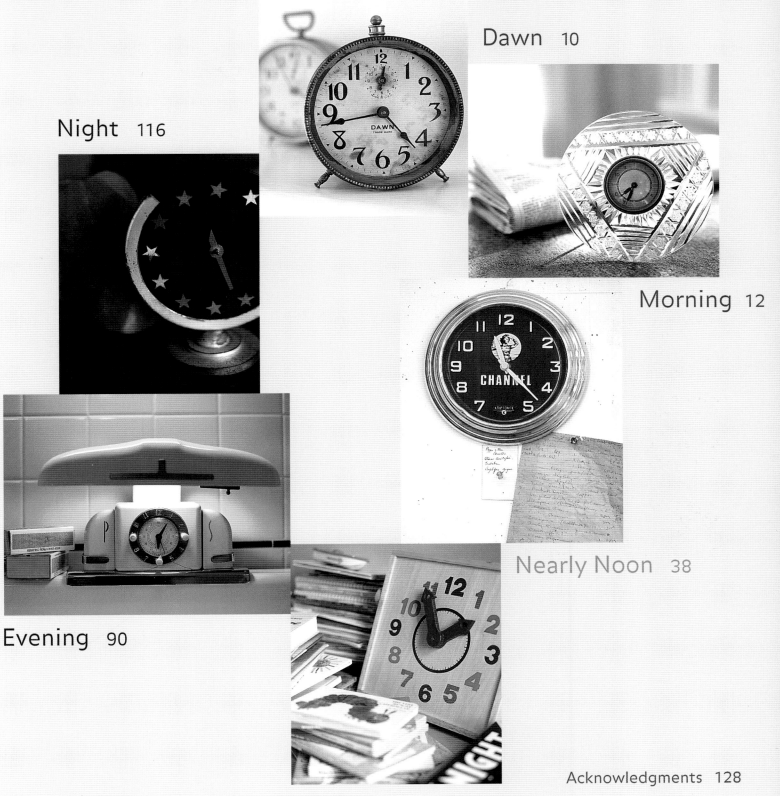

If the little hand is on the eight and the big hand is on the twelve, what time is it?

Do you remember the triumph, the magic of that moment as a child when you first solved the mystery of time; when that jumble of numbers and the movement of little hands and big hands suddenly made such perfect sense? Maybe you were taught with one of those bright, colorful toy clocks. When you pushed the hands with the tips of your fingers, you could see the gears, the wheels behind the face as they turned around and around. Eight o' clock. Time to get up. Twelve o' clock. Time for lunch. Six o'clock. Time for dinner. In learning how to tell time, you acquired a degree of mastery over it. You were no longer at its mercy. It had meaning.

Like the rooms we inhabited as children, rooms so clearly defined by a traditional purpose or function, the movement of time at home added a reassuring element of certainty and predictability to everyday life. Even if it could no longer be manipulated as easily as the big and little hands of a toy clock, its precision helped establish boundaries, the boundaries with which you would eventually define yourself and the world around you.

Today, with the whole concept of boundaries fast becoming as blurred as the flicker of flight numbers in a departure lounge, and time itself a luxury few if any of us possess, that world of childhood probably feels as far away as the future did then, or as the nearly defunct tick tock of an old-fashioned Big Ben clock. (Remember how the tick tock seemed as loud as the clock the crocodile swallowed in Peter Pan?)

We now live in a world of the perpetual present, a world where that old-fashioned tick tock has been replaced by the beep of a pager, fax, or cell phone, by the click of a mouse and the screech of what novelist J. G. Ballard calls "electronic angels" as we impatiently wait for our modems to connect us with a world more wired than we are. It is a world defined by a new kind of windows. A world without walls so incredibly small, some of us actually pilot our way in and around it from an object that fits in the palm of our hands.

Although many of the rituals and routines we first associated with time at home remain the same, the distance between that outside and our inside world seems to be vanishing. Not just virtually, but literally. Our homes, for instance, are no longer just where the heart is but often where the office is, too. Rooms once defined (and confined) by a single purpose or function now serve many. We chat, trade, even shop around the clock. But as the lines that once separated inside from outside, public from private, work from play, and day from night grow finer and finer, time at home only becomes more precious. More meaningful.

Our homes are a product of time. They are created not by the dizzying speed of digital connections but by the intimacy of emotional connections; not by fiber-optic links and satellite signals but by the impulse and power of personal passions and memories. It is the vividness, the intensity, of these personal passions and memories, matched with an occasional flight of fantasy and imagination, that keep us in touch with what is real, and that help us stay grounded in a world without boundaries.

Why did the man throw the clock out the window? Because he wanted to see time fly.

What is it about this joke, this attempt to grasp the elusiveness, the abstractness, of time, that still makes children giggle? Grown-ups, of course, know that time flies the fastest when looking back at the past—when flipping through a family album and seeing photographs of grandparents, of weddings and honeymoons, or of kids who've grown up and gone away. But think of how many other ways our emotions help define and measure the impact of time at home.

Think of how heavy its weight when we worry about the rising fever of a child but how light when we laugh; when we enjoy the company of friends at a dinner that lasts long after the last candle has smoldered and flickered out. Think of how time seems to stop, how slowly it drifts along when we're in a hurry or forced into the idleness of waiting; and of how the body itself, the rhythms of mood and desire, also help measure the meaning and momentum of time, this force that remains otherwise invisible, unseen.

Now think of how we rely on the senses, on sight, sound, even smell, to help us identify particular times of day and night. Think of dawn: the cry of a newborn baby, a ripple of birdsong, the grinding of gears in a garbage truck. Then the tantalizing aroma of freshly brewed coffee. Of burnt toast. There's also the murmur of a radio, the sound of rushing water, and the ghosts of mist in a morning shower. These are a just a few of the cues of half-remembered vitality that bring us back to life every day. Think of the snip, snip, the clip of gardening shears in late afternoon, or the crunch of tires on a gravel driveway and the slam of a car door that for a child signals the long awaited arrival of a parent home from work. Or the creak of wood, the gentle hissing, and the banging of pipes as the bones of a house settle themselves into sleep for the night.

Many of us have a natural-born affinity for specific times of day or night; times when we feel most in synch, not just with the self and with who we are but with the world around us. For some, it may be that tiny island of solitude when the sunlight first splinters through the shadows of dawn; when it is no longer night but not quite day and the rest of the house is still caught in a tangle of sheets and last-minute dreams. For others, it's that rush of adrenaline on an early morning run before the first cup of coffee, the bright glare of noon, the softening of light as it fades into a sky streaked with red at dusk, or the cover of night when the dazzle of darkness holds true to its promise of privacy.

Whether it is the sudden surfacing of our subconscious, of memory, or some inexplicable impulse that creates this synchrony is almost irrelevant. These particular affinities play as pivotal and spirited a role in transforming a house into a home as our choice of furnishings, paint, fabric, and decor.

As for these hugely significant and very personal choices. . . . Here again, it is our connection with time (and all it implies) that seems to be of the essence. Why, for instance, are some of us irresistibly attracted to the rigorous discipline of everything that is modern and minimalist, while others embrace the ornate decoration and cozy clutter of the Victorians? What about the sophisticated allure of Art Deco and the 1930s, the nostalgia for the retro 1950s, the craftsmanship of the Early American years, and the distant gilded echoes of Europe in its Golden Ages?

Perhaps, the birth and nurturing of these passions for various periods reflect a longing to be one with time; for a sense of continuity. Like the patina of an heirloom grandfather clock, a patina that emerges only after generations of hands before us have gently rubbed and buffed its surface, the proximity of these connections to the past, present, and even the future remind us that nothing and no one is ever truly gone or forgotten.

More ephemeral or transient than the senses, passion, and memory is the thought that every home is a world onto itself. Within that world, there are usually certain corners or places that seem to call out to us; to speak to us over time. Maybe it's that favorite old armchair near an open window, the seclusion of an upstairs bedroom, or a busy, crowded kitchen. No matter where they are located, these are the places we seek out with an almost instinctual sense of both comfort and return. Not once or twice but over and over again. They are places that form the image and the very definition of home.

Just think of a book half opened on its spine. It sits on the seat of that favorite armchair in a dim pool of light. The lamp on the nearby table is on and there is a pile of luggage in the hallway nearby. Whether this image speaks of that blissfully quiet interlude snatched before leaving a house or the sleepy fatigue of arriving, there is within this single moment of time, this intimacy interrupted, a story.

Time At Home is devoted to exploring these stories. As we at Echo have discovered, every home is furnished with an almost infinite number of these isolated moments, moments that together create a truly unique picture of how each and every one of us chooses to bring time to life at home. Far from solving the mystery of time, we hope these images and stories offer a means of "seeing," perhaps, even feeling time in a new and unexpected light.

DAWN

The moment the sunlight splinters through the shadows, the essence of gentle awakenings

MORNING

The ripple of birdsong,

the murmur of a shower radio,

the tantalizing aroma

of freshly brewed coffee

A Clean Start

Like the rush of water in an early morning shower, emerging from the sluggishness of sleep into the silvery sparkle of this perfectly appointed bathroom invigorates body and soul.

Splash!

Airing the Bed

Navigating the Dawn

A Favorite Time of Day: When it is no longer night and not quite day,
and the rest of the house is still caught up in a tangle of sheets
and last-minute dreams.

Once upon a Time

In a bedroom as pristinely white and innocent
as newborn life, an infant's early morning cries
are soothed and quieted.

Islands of the Morning

Backpacks are loaded,
oatmeal is served.

Happy Home Making

This kitchen, with its witty allusions to the 1950s
and the great American diner, is a uniquely cheerful spot
for eating eggs over easy.

Pitcher Perfect

Pillows Talk

Cushioned with pillows in stripes, solids, and luscious florals and decorated with vintage mercury glass and primitive paintings, this room clearly speaks of the beauty and joy of creating a very personal space.

Room to Grow

Time seems almost suspended in this child's fantasy of white picket fences, blue skies, flower-strewn meadows, and friendly wildlife.

25

Time Together

Gathering on the weekend for a big family breakfast with a second-generation high chair and a flea-market folding bench reminds us that our furnishings, like families, evolve over time.

Fern Fresh

Bathing in this old-fashioned tub with room enough to wiggle one's toes and windows wide open makes bathing pure pleasure.

Morning Ablution

Mixed Media

The black varnished wooden floors, ponyskin rug, and bouquet of branches echoed in the spindly twiglike legs of a round table create a bedroom both stark and soothing. Light from the unshaded windows and the plump dog bed on the floor serve to soften harsh edges.

"Light" Work and Solitary Pleasures

Wicker, wood, and lots of lacquered white offer a
glimpse of how simple morning routines like laundry
and straightening the kitchen can be seen as rituals
that help restore a sense of order and well-being
to everyday living.

Baby and Me

The kids are off to school, the baby has been fed and is napping,
and the house is all yours—for the moment.

Home Economics

This ingenious marriage of living, sleeping, and occasional work space shows just how cleverly today's multitaskers can make an intensely personal statement in even the smallest, most economically sized city studio.

Black Light

There's nothing shy or timid about this design decision. As dramatic as it is serene, the singular contrast of black and white in this twin bedroom may be strong enough to inspire dreams in color.

Do Not Disturb

Nothing seems to intrude or disturb the peacefulness of this meticulously modern bedroom space. With its wrought-iron bedstead neatly framed by two windows, even the room's horizontal blinds add to the feeling of precision and orderly comfort.

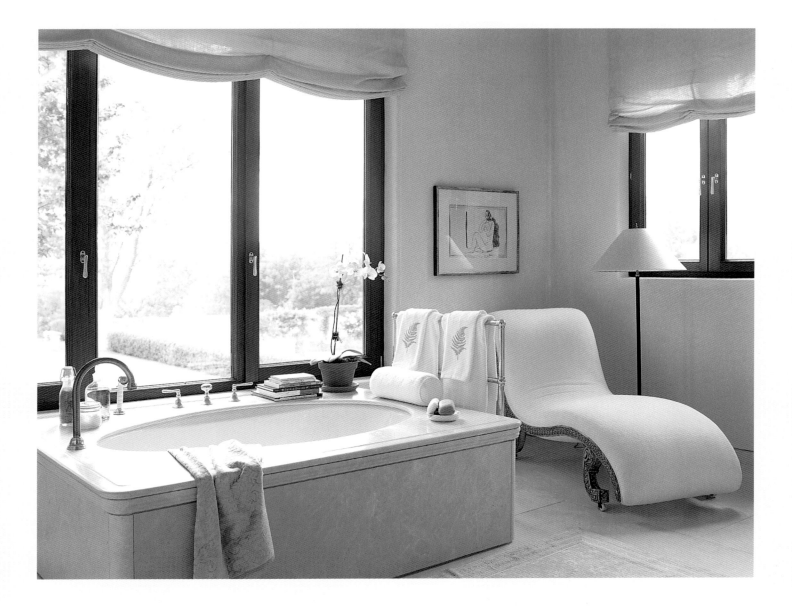

Spa Time

Hats On, Lights Off
This vision of mismatched twin beds
and reading lamps shaded with old
straw hats evokes the world of secrets
and friendship shared by sisters,
a bond that only grows stronger
and more profound over time.

NEARLY NOON

Home is where the hearth is,

its heart and soul

Home Portals

In a world with fewer and fewer borders and no transitional time,
the traditional porch continues to mark the boundaries
between the inside and outside world, and public and private lives.
An old cast-iron hen stands guard outside the house.

High Noon

Time Warp
The blissful marriage of today and yesterday: telecommuting
from an eighteenth-century stone house with old-fashioned
wooden beams and floors makes the reality of working at home
a privilege and a pleasure.

Berry, Berry Red

Press Enter

Paying bills, catching up on phone calls, transferring your Rolodex onto a Palm Pilot. It's all a breeze in this neat corner office, perched on the edge of a living room and surrounded by real (versus virtual) windows.

Canary Island

Radiant, glazed yellow tiles with matching yellow island and antique canisters above the stove are in perfect synchrony with the sunlight that streams in over the kitchen sink.

Primary Colors

Family Game Plan

The Self: Contained
The fascinating cross-section of floors
built into the architecture of this country
home acts as a brilliant metaphor for the
multidimensional lives we lead.

Space Shuttling

This spacious kitchen with its shiny chrome and steel surfaces
mirrors a taste for millenium modern. A click of the remote control
from the work station and you can learn to make a fabulous fish dinner
while balancing your checkbook.

Upwardly Noble (and Mobile)

With its glass-paned doors, wooden table on wheels, and chairs sitting on the slenderest of spiderlike legs, this room says as much about the lightness of being as it does about the art of maximizing and expanding upon the feeling of spaciousness.

Cool Cubist

The juxtaposition of snow whites against white is punctuated by the slivers of black frames and a favorite nineteenth-century Indian armoire.

Comfort Zone

12 o'clock High

The ceiling skylight funnels sunlight directly
into this artist's studio and living space.
With its vivid eye-popping use of color
and casual layering of new and truly ancient
(sometimes priceless) objects, this room
is as civilized as it is intensely personal
and comfortable.

A/R

(Artist in Residence)

If you lived here, you'd be home right now
Sometimes, there is no place in the world as intriguing, as promising, even as adventurous as one's own backyard.

Time Out

Eastern
Mountain Time
Bunk beds made and half-
made with antique Beacon
blankets are a reminder of
lazy, summer days spent at
the family cabin.

Coming Home
The handy catch-all room is for dropping tennis rackets, soccer
balls, boots, you name it. Every house should have one.

AFTERNOON

When the natural rhythms

of mood and desire

help measure the meaning

and the momentum of time

Golden Hour

Works in Progress

More than just an artist's studio, this room with
its controlled chaos offers a sublime example of
how a transfusion of midday light and color
transforms still images into something as moving
and inspiring as a finished canvas.

Colorforms
The deep blue corner of a city loft space with its Caldersesque floor lamp, postmodern toddlers' toys, gilded picture frames, and comfy slipcovered armchair is the epitome of not just elegance but eccentric ease.

Graphic Arts
Carefully orchestrated and beautifully functional, this kitchen with its bright white walls and designer chairs, dark stained wooden table, and pegged floors is made for the joys of cooking. (Not to mention afternoon snacking with Oreos and milk.)

Natural Skylight

This fantasy of bright Indian plaids and striped silk-and-cotton pillows on a nineteenth-century canopy bed that is open to the embrace of nature and the sky seems perfectly in place, even outside.

Clean Getaway

There is a certain euphoria one associates with showering outdoors. It is a sensation as liberating as it is captivating and a moment that conjures up the exhilaration and freedom of youth.

Moving Out
(Without Leaving Home)

Sheer Joy

It's Just a Summer Shower

A breeze is blowing in through the open window. You're just back from a hot afternoon at the beach and it's time to shower the sand off your feet.

In the Pink

There is something almost illicit in the pleasures of surrendering to
drowsiness and a short, afternoon nap; of taking a break before the
kids are home from school and sinking into sleep in this pool of pink lit
by a shaft of golden afternoon sun.

Point of View

Afternoon Playdate

Every girl loves having friends over after school and hiding away in her own room. With its Early American wooden bed, "private" armchair and ottoman, and checkerboard-painted floor, this room is tailor made for sharing a love for dogs, dolls, and stuffed animals.

Postcards on the Edge

Souvenirs and mementos from other times and places traveled.

A World onto Itself

If every house is a world onto itself, there are certain places within that world, such as a favorite armchair near an open window, that seem to call out to us over time. They are places we seek out with a reassuring sense of both comfort and return.

The Last Word

Finishing the crossword puzzle on a quiet Sunday afternoon is easy going on this daybed covered in the stripes of antique ticking. It is a rare moment when time itself seems to stop.

Old Glory

Flagging spirits are revived in this niche with a down pillow and shawl created for spontaneous napping or relaxing.

A Study in Contrasts

An Early American milk-painted hutch holds a collection of
everything from stones worn with age and the touch of human
hands to photographs and baskets. Wooden floors, bookcases,
and a chaise longue upholstered in white canvas make this
study a timeless classic.

Time Laps

It's 3:30. And you've just finished your thirty laps. You feel as placid as the mirrorlike surface of the pool, a pool that seems to have sprung as naturally from the landscape as the stone house (for changing, maybe even napping) drenched in foliage behind it.

Open House

Here, down-filled sofas in muted shades of beige and gray provide a natural foil for the forest of greenery outside "invisible" walls of windows. With the shine of steely metal surfaces softened by changes in sunlight, this is a living room that is environmentally friendly in every sense of the word.

Afternoon Book Club

The airiness and artful display of meaningful objects, such as
the collection of modern photographs and the sketch on an easel,
add to this room's sense of character and nonchalant ease.

The Piano Lesson

Teen Dream

Whether they're into hip-hop, heavy metal, or just discovering the Beatles, this teenage retreat on the third floor is perfect for all of their far from trivial pursuits. (It's also far enough away from grown-ups to make even the loudest jamming and spinning soundproof.)

Cool Pool

Chef's Special

The warm honey-colored kitchen table, antique burnished copper cooking pots, and sentinel-like parade of glass canisters on a shelf is a cook's dream, ready for baking muffins and cookies on a rainy spring afternoon or preparing the ultimate gourmet meal.

AtHomeAtWorkAtHomeAtWork

EVENING

The turn of a key,

the anticipation of return,

the warmth of a ready meal—

home at last

At a farmhouse table with
rustic leather chairs, food
for thought is served
together with casual
and more formal meals.

Book Bound

Re-Entry Point

A perfect interim space not only for dropping keys, agenda, and mail but for keeping track of the comings and goings that mark the movement of time at home.

Ready, Set

Cabin Fever
Lighting a fire as the sun sets reignites weary spirits and helps mark
that change of mood from day into evening.

Home Work

As compact and cozy as a ship's cabin, this efficiently organized
but highly personalized office space is neatly tucked away
in the back of the house and makes light work of last-minute
phone calls and faxing before cocktails.

Mirror Mirror (not just on the wall)

The Invisible Hands of Time

A glorious antique Lalique crystal clock sits in the
very center of a collection of highly prized glass
vases behind a deep, dark red velvet sofa.
This voluptuous and divinely decadent room is
definitely made for adults only.

The Everlasting Cool of White

There is no question that this is the room of a woman who makes time for the bliss and the luxury of solitude. Seductively pure in its use of color, form, and function, it is the product of a truly discriminating eye.

Seeing Spots

More like polka dots. Hand painted by the owner, this mantlepiece sheds a whole new light on the delights of a fireplace.

A Little More Bubbly

Soaking away tension and daytime pressures in a twilight
bubble bath with aromatic candles is a necessary indulgence—
one of life's little, indispensable luxuries.

Inner Sanctum

As a moment of reflection and revelation, the pleasures of dressing up
are hardly lost with age. They are pleasures that involve a transformation.
Here, every detail is perfect: from the gown and shoes laid out in the
back, to the discreetly shaded lamps on the vanity table, to the generously
sized closets and mirror.

Bright Lights, Very Big City

White Nights

Silver Polished

Think of how the simple act of turning on a lamp at the end of day, of touching familiar objects on a favorite hallway table, reorients the senses and brings one safely back home.

Safe Haven

Like Vesta, the Roman goddess of the hearth, a female bust gracefully watches over a living room that feels extraordinarily warm and comfortable.

Time Honored

Like the patina of an heirloom clock, our connections to the past, present, and even the future remind us that nothing and no one is truly forgotten.

Paris (and other worlds) by Night

Classical renderings of architectural landmarks are mixed with a three-dimensional model of the Tour Eiffel, a haphazardly stacked pile of books, and designer lamps from the 1930s and '40s to create a niche as attuned to the past as it is to the present.

109

Animal Kingdom
Soft shades of beige and green and uncreased white linens
seem to suggest that insomnia never happens here.

Urbane Safari
With its leopard-spotted
stairway and silver Razor
scooter, this is a foyer
that defines the nature
of everything that is
city sleek and chic.

Profile in Courage

An unlikely and fearless combination of colors, textures, and objects proves that risks are well worth taking.

Through the Looking Glass

This breathtakingly dramatic living room first captures attention through a brilliant use of color and contrast, while leading the eye through a looking glass, into other worlds.

Day is Done

NIGHT

Easing from the daytime
world into the mysterious
realm of darkness

Go with the Glow

Here, in a party scene as spectacular as a Hollywood set, the glow goes on after the rays of the sun have gone.

That's Entertainment

Think of how the emotions help measure the weight of time. Think of how light its weight when we laugh and enjoy the company of friends at a dinner that lasts long after the last candle has smoldered and flickered out.

Early Retirement

A hand-stenciled doorway, painted wood-paneled walls, and the casual arrangement of family portraits and photographs create an artful but unpretentious corner that is both alive to the present and enamored with the past.

9:30 PM

Imagine sipping a quiet brandy and turning the pages of the latest
thriller or best-selling biography in this formally structured but warm
and enticing library.

Fireside Chat

The sense of enclosure and intimacy in the den of this country house is enhanced by the fire glowing in the hearth and the unorthodox marriage of textures: leather, wood, and stone.

A Moment of Illumination

Even the stairway seems to invite one upstairs to bed.

Book Worm

With books at the head and all around the bed and an old framed map, this is a room that speaks of a passion for reading as well as late-night armchair traveling and meandering.

Midnight Snack

Dazzle of Darkness

An exotic Raj-inspired bedroom keeps true to its promise of privacy.

Midnight Oil

The melding of stars and
shadows seems all
enveloping as the house
settles itself in for
a good night's sleep.

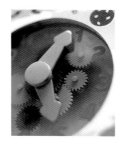

ACKNOWLEDGMENTS

We are so pleased to have been given the opportunity to create a second home decorative book. With it came many new challenges; tackling them was made much easier by assembling what we think was a remarkable team. We were once again privileged to be able to work with the incredibly talented Maura McEvoy and Brenda Cullerton. Maura's beautiful photographs are a result of not only her unerring artistic eye and technical ability but also her sensitivity and dedication to this project. Brenda's tremendous intelligence and wit are evidenced in the inspired text, and we thank her for the enthusiasm and global vision that helped to shape our notion of *Time at Home*.

New to our team was Henk van Assen, who graphically brought the words and photos together with his very thoughtful and intelligent book design.

Time at Home would not have been possible without the support of the people at Echo. Diane Baker, Echo's Licensing Director, went far beyond the call of duty in her devotion to this project. She not only took care of all administrative details, but on location was a gofer, mover, cleaner, flower stylist, and wallpaper hanger, and even risked injury in a rosebush for the sake of a photograph! We are fortunate to have family members who are talented, caring, helpful, and in the business. Dot and Lynn Roberts, principals at Echo, and Amy Lesser Courage, an architect and interior designer, were always available as "in-house consultants" on all aspects of the book; Michelle Blume and Sara Goldberg made it possible for the home division to continue to function during the demanding book production schedule.

Tremendous thanks go to all those who contributed so much creativity and energy assisting us in styling the photo shoots. Jeanne-Aelia Desparmet-Hart was at nearly every location and brought not only her special design talents but also a wonderful positive spirit. We also thank Bruce Glickman and Amy Kaiser Wickersham, who each provided their unique design sensibilities at critical times.

We want to thank our wonderful licensing partners, F. Schumacher & Co., Revman Industries, C.R. Gibson, Kravet Fabrics, and Mallory & Church for providing product at a moment's notice.

We are again extremely grateful to all of the people who so generously and graciously opened their homes to us: Melanie Acevedo and Richard White, Linda Allard, Christine Armstrong and Ben Nickoll, Donald and Shawna Barrett, Loraine Bauchmann, Jon Carloftis, Eileen and Fred Cohen, Laurin Copen, David DeNicolo and Stephen Ketterer, Jeanne-Aelia and Steve Hart, Sandi and John Fifield, Donna Francis and Richard Pierce, Katja Goldman and Michael Sonnenfeldt, Page Goolrick, Susan Hager, Michael Johnston, Christine Lambert and Robert Layton, Lark and Rick Levine, Claudia Librett, Margery and Ted Mayer, Maura McEvoy and Steven Wagner, Denise and Francis Menton, Steve Miller, James and Amanda Moffat, Paula and Steven Morvay, Jennifer Pendry, Susan and Mark Romney, Dennis Samuels, Lisa and Michael Schwartzman, Joyce and James Seymore, Francois Simard, Elaine Stimmel, Amy and John Wickersham, and Eileen and Carter Wiseman.

We would like to thank several terrific people who gave so much time and thought to this project behind the scenes. They either helped us find great locations or assisted us once we arrived: William Boyd, Francie Campbell, Ginny Edwards, Sandi Fifield, Carolyn Klemm of Klemm Real Estate, Yves Landry, Karen Loomis, and Elaine Stimmel of Dayton-Halstead Realty.

We can't thank enough all our friends at Abrams who have been so supportive of our first book and enthusiastically encouraged us to proceed with a second. We especially thank our editor, Elisa Urbanelli, for her guidance and expertise. Elisa was always there when we needed her and made this gigantic undertaking a truly pleasurable experience.

Last, but certainly not least, we thank our children Sam, Charlie, and Lily—the reasons we cherish our time at home.